Shoveling Mud into Rushing Water

CL Bledsoe

Poems in this manuscript previously appeared in similar forms in the following journals:

Arkansas Literary Forum, Arkansas Review, Atticus Review, The Avenue, Bluestone Review, Cahaba River Literary Journal, Concho River Review, Dead Snakes, Emerge Literary Journal, Flint Hills, Floodwall, Foliate Oak, Fourth & Sycamore, Fried Chicken and Coffee, Gravel, Hobo Camp Review, Ilya's Honey, Kentucky Review, Loch Raven Review, The McNeese Review, Nebo, The Olive Press, Open Letters Monthly, Poetry Quarterly, Red Eft Review, Revolution John, Right Hand Pointing, San Pedro River Review, Semaphore Magazine, Slant, Tell-Tale Inklings, Tipton Poetry Journal, Toasted Cheese, Town Creek Poetry, Tulane Review, Two Cities Review, White Ash Literary Magazine, Windward Review

"A Cloud of Blackbirds" and "The Grass in Arkansas" were selected for the 2017 *Number One* award for poetry.

"A Cloud of Blackbirds" was also nominated for the Pushcart Prize by *Ilya's Honey*.

Contents

VACATION 7

HUNTINGTON'S DISEASE 8

FUNNEL CLOUD 9

THE SLOUGH 10

FIRST HAIRCUT 11

SOMETHING FOR NOTHING 12

SOMETHING ABOUT LIGHTNING AND
A YOUNG GIRL'S HEART 13

FREE RANGE 15

FLAGGING 16

SHOVELING MUD INTO RUSHING WATER 17

DIANA 18

GOING TO SEE MOM 19

THE GOLD MINE 20

SUNDAY 21

CAT'S HEAD BISCUITS AND CHOCOLATE GRAVY 22

GOOD INTENTIONS 23

DWI 24

BREAD CRUMBS 25

LEVEES ALWAYS LEAK 26

I NEVER DID 27

STRAW 28

CUTTING BULLS 29

THE NEW POND 30

THE FIRST TIME 32

RED 33

CANTALOUPE 34

SEINING 35

COWS ARE OUT 36

ETIQUETTE 37

HOW TO RECYCLE A FARM TRUCK 38

THE FISH SHACK 39
13 WAYS OF LOOKING AT A RICE FIELD 40
MUD 42
IT WAS QUIET, THERE 43
HE NEVER BOTHERED ME AGAIN 44
COWS 45
TEA 46
WAR WITH KOREA 47
A BOY AND HIS DOG 48
WE NAMED HIM SMEAGOL BECAUSE OF HIS BUG EYES 49
THE PATH 50
JOHNSON'S FREEZE INN 51
FROGBALL 52
HARD TIMES, ARKANSAS 53
HONORS ENGLISH 54
GUARDIANS 55
THIRSTY 56
MY FATHER, DRIVING 57
WALLOW 59
Doing His Best 60
SHOES 61
THE WATER MOCCASIN'S MOUNTAIN 62
WHITE BEANS 63
THE WIZARD 65
THE ONE-EYED KING'S LAMENT 66
WALMART 67
TO THE POLICEMAN WHO CALLED ME MA'AM 69
HUFFING POTPOURRI WHILE LISTENING TO TOOL 70
NIGHTS WERE LONG 71
I WAS THIN, THEN, AND YOUNG 72
THE YELLOW KING 73
NEW YEAR'S DAY 74
SWEATER 75
EVERYTHING I KNOW ABOUT CHICKENS 76
GRANDMA OKRA 78

HOW TO COOK SQUIRREL 79
AFTER HE SOBERED UP 80
A CLOUD OF BLACKBIRDS 82
THE GRASS IN ARKANSAS 83
ELVIS 84
THE LESSON 85
JACKSON 86
CROSSWORD 88
STRENGTH 89
MUSIC 90

VACATION

The mound of trash bags in the back
of the station wagon meant we weren't

coming back. In Missouri, Uncle Don
had a piano we couldn't touch and a barn full

of newborn puppies we could see when he
was sure he could trust us. My sister wouldn't

stop crying, so they locked us in the basement
to watch TV. That night, she snuck into

the bathroom and tried to figure out which
of Mom's pills would kill her and which

would just make her sick. She'd be alone, then,
never to see Dad or our brother again.

HUNTINGTON'S DISEASE

Mom sat on the edge of her bed, crying,
"I'm sick. I'm sick." Dad said it was all
in her head and stayed out later each night,
drinking with his buddies he hated. So much
has been lost. The things she used to say
when she talked to herself. The first time she
discovered vanilla. Did Jesus help her,
or were we wasting time at church eight days
a week? No one sat us down and explained:
your mother is dying badly. Something more
important was always happening, the cows
were out, or the rice was scorching at
the Johnson place. There were stories about
her Dad, unable to walk but strong enough
to punch a dent into his car on the way to
the nursing home. His mother no one talked
about. They called it Huntington's Chorea,
which made me think one of my uncles brought
it back from the war, but meant dance. Imagine
the Holy Spirit stole your body– I'd seen it
in tent revivals, twitching parishioners
mumble-screaming nonsense. The difference
for them was at the end, they got theirs back.

FUNNEL CLOUD

Lightning crackles, illuminating the dark
clouds, swirling black and purple, blue
and gray. My sister and I, all scabby knees

and elbows, propped on our parents'
bed, watch the churning air. The cloud dips
at the bottom of the hill, sprouts a trunk

that reaches for the ground in hunger,
but withdraws, finding only dirt. The gyre
spins, rises back into the air and moves

closer. The lightning is gone. We see
nothing but dark until a white crash reveals
the whirling dervish just outside the window

with a delicious tremble, stretching down, buoyed
by the wind. It passes above us, out of sight.
Darkness settles outside again full of grumbling

thunder, chattering rain, violence we can't name.
Somewhere behind us, a crash.

THE SLOUGH

Dad made the mistake of leaving my sister
alone in the truck while he went to check
on the integrity of the rice levees. She waited
a good fifteen minutes before she put on
adult-sized boots, waded out after him,
and got stuck in the saturated soil.

They say you can dive underwater
and a moccasin will pass overhead,
but when she saw one slither across the top
of the water, she didn't bother testing
this hypothesis and instead set to hollering
until dad returned, neatly chopped
the thing in half with his shovel, yanked
her free and carried her back to the truck.

This time, she stayed only five before
climbing out and finding a slough on the edge
of the field exploding with thousands of baby
frogs. That's where he found her, some
time later, looking up at him with big dark
eyes and offering him a tiny frog in her hand.

FIRST HAIRCUT

Mom loved my long, blond locks. Dad
thought I looked like a girl. He waited

as long as he could stand, until the tresses
reached my shoulders, snatched

me up, and took me to the barber shop
downtown. A man I didn't know helped

me up onto the booster on his chair
with a smile. When I cried because Mom

had cried, he tried to convince Dad
it was okay to wait. But Dad

insisted, and I left looking like a boy.
It wasn't long after that my hair darkened

from Mom's blond to Dad's raven
black stain.

SOMETHING FOR NOTHING

There were plates and bowls, crockery
with little yellow and blue daisies
on them. Every week, IGA had a different
piece. They gave out stamps when
you bought enough. When the vacuum
broke, Mom saved the stamps in her little
book. She had to take them all the way
to the mall in Jonesboro. Dad said,
"You can't get something for nothing."
Mom said, "It's not nothing." He
wouldn't take her until she threatened
to go by herself. On the hour drive up,
he repeated, "You can't get something
for nothing." On the drive back, the vacuum
sat in the back seat, quiet as Dad up front.

SOMETHING ABOUT LIGHTNING AND A YOUNG GIRL'S HEART

1

Her favorite tree was a giant old pecan halfway
down the south face of the shaggy hill, between
the red brick house and the stock pond. Lightning
silenced it, but after it stumbled its last, fell soft
and slow, she stayed loyal, playing in the cave
of its hollowed husk until Dad found out about
the black snakes hiding in the too-long grass
and ran her off with stories that they'd catch
a scent and chase her for miles.

2

Her second favorite tree was over behind
the house by the mini cliff where the boys
from the neighborhood below came to throw
dirt-clod grenades at each other. Before lightning
got that one, she used to catch frogs there.
She'd put them in an empty mayonnaise jar,
leave it in the utility room overnight. Every morning,
Dad would let them go. She could never explain
the lonesome job she'd given herself to civilize them.

3

Her third favorite tree shed its pecans halfway
up the gravel road that led to the fork at the top
of the ridge. She liked to hear them crunch
under dad's tires. The road snaked up the narrow
ridge with grass falling off to either side,
and a worn cattle trail left it, descending down
to the tree. This one lasted years before the lightning
split it, burned it to the ground in two days. She cried
like it was family and moped around until
wildflowers grew from its corpse in vibrant blues,
yellows, greens, and reds. Dad would never admit
to planting them, but they reminded her
of Mamaw's garden, gone these last several years.

FREE RANGE

My sister and I rode in the back
of Dad's filthy truck, with the empty
beer cans, the grease and dirt, tailgate
long gone; we'd take turns jumping out
on the shoulder, chase the slow-moving
truck, and dive back in. Sometimes,
I'd grab her shoe and throw it so she'd
have to hop down after it. Sometimes,
we'd push each other out. Once, I jumped
as Dad was pulling onto the highway, skinned
knees on the asphalt, and limped as fast
as I could to reach my sister, laughing
too hard to stretch out a hand to help me.
Dad never saw me, or made out like he hadn't,
but I caught him at a red light before
he got out of town. Maybe there were buckles
shoved back under the seat somewhere,
but who wanted to ride up front anyway
where you couldn't feel the breeze?

FLAGGING

The engine buzz was a never-ending giant
mosquito always hovering just behind my ear.
I had to hold the orange flag steady and high

so the duster could see it, but I also had to clear
out before he started laying down the insecticide.
He'd come in low and spray, and as soon

as I heard him dive, I'd move to the next rows
of soybeans. We hadn't had time to plant the flags
to guide him, so we had to do it by hand. I was slow

the first pass and got showered with little white pellets.
Dad said it would make me grow a third arm and offered
me a beer to rinse the chemical taste from my mouth.

SHOVELING MUD INTO RUSHING WATER

Dad dragged me along to fetch
things I couldn't carry. I'd push
ratty sneakers down into rubber boots

so they'd mostly fit, the tops like wide-
mouthed lizards swallowing my legs,
and sloosh out into the rice fields after

him. Anything was better than sitting
in the truck, eyes burning from the OFF!
that didn't help. It was cooler in the water.

With a shovel on my back and the couple
spills I could carry, if I stopped, I'd come
out of a boot, have to balance on one leg,

and then stab my foot back down; he
wouldn't wait. By the time I tottered
to the broke levee, he was already on his

second shovelful. I pushed in, the curved
brown metal sliding soft and then so heavy,
I could barely lift it to splash into the hole

where water rushed out. The mud washed
away as I watched. "Keep going," Dad said.
"Always keep going."

DIANA

Warrior princess at five years old, a bath towel
safety-pinned around her neck to billow as she dashed

through the house in scuffed white sneakers, blown-out-
knee jeans, and a county fair tee shirt. Pursued

by a furious Hippolyta yelling to quit running in
and out of the kitchen while I'm canning preserves!

She vaulted out the front door, over the steps, landed
in quaking grass on one knee, then rose, ready

for evildoers, be they ninja, robot, or school teacher.
When Wonder Woman cracked her Lasso of Truth,

fathers couldn't promise they'd be home early but roll
in loaded, late, and ready to fight. Mothers

couldn't spend all day watching soap operas while
their deific daughters ran wild and bored. Her golden

bracelets deflected ballistic language shot from cruel
lips. Her tiara could cut through the mundaneness

of any day. An Amazonian warrior needed no help
from any man; only the goddesses who granted

her strength. From her invisible plane, perched
in the pecan tree's shedding limbs, she could look

down on the weak world while no one could see her.

GOING TO SEE MOM

We stopped at a Tastee Freeze and Dad
ordered a chili dog, which was so at odds
with his usual palate that to this day, I can't
reconcile it. We stopped outside of St. Louis
at a motel that was decent mostly because Dad
wasn't savvy enough to find one cheaper.
It had a Godzilla movie on TV and all the ice
you could eat. When we got to Grandmother's
house, it was us vs. them, and I was squarely
in the Dad camp with my sister, my brother,
seemingly the whole world. Grandmother
said I was too dirty to sit, so I stood. Mom
was broken. She'd lost her family and was staring
down the barrel of a future whose ending
she'd seen. Soon, she would lose herself
to the disease that took her father, his mother.
She stood there, the saddest thing you ever
saw, knew my sister, no one was going to hug
her or even pretend to be happy, poisoned
as we'd been against her. She just smiled at us.
My brother, behind me, unnoticed, shoved me,
hard. My arms flew out and found her.
We clung to each other for life.

THE GOLD MINE

Signs exist for a reason. This one, a massive
once-white piece of plywood, dotted
with potshots, sagged above the levee holding
the water in the big stock pond we called
The Lake. Maybe it said No Hunting, maybe
some kind of warning, but my sister got it
in her head it marked the now-collapsed
entrance to a gold mine. She'd imagined there
was one not too far away, and if the president
won't tell the truth about what was found
on the dark side of the moon, why would anyone
admit a spur of precious metal rested just
underneath our pasture? The plan was to convince
me and our cousin Scott to dig. Or course, we
were all too young for shovels, so we used
spoons. We dug for hours, found a shark's
tooth and no gold. After three days, mom
got mad about the dirty spoons and forbade us
from going back over by the pond. My sister
made a new plan: to dig a pool in the front
yard, line it with trash bags. Maybe we'd strike oil.

SUNDAY

Behind a wooden alter, white-robed old
men who smelled like fried chicken lectured

us about the sins of our minds. A pool
of greenish-blue water stagnated beside them.

They claimed it held the secrets to our salvation,
if only we'd let them dip us in with their shaking

arms. When the singing woke us, we begged
to go to the bathroom, and searched the otherwise

empty building. We explored every door, climbed
to the balcony looking for something worth finding

while in the other room, our neighbors
smiled politely and damned us to hell.

CAT'S HEAD BISCUITS AND CHOCO-LATE GRAVY

I only had it one time, when I was
a boy. I was playing down the hill
with cousin John. Aunt Jo Ann,
his grandmother, announced she
would make chocolate gravy. It seemed
like a bad idea. I didn't know
how to make gravy so I didn't know
how chocolate gravy was any different,
except that she added cocoa powder
to it. But gravy needs a vessel,
which means she had to make–
homemade, lard and flour– cat's head
biscuits, called that because when you
break them off to cook them, they resemble
a cat's head. You didn't need butter,
just tore them in half and she'd ladle
some gravy over top. She told me not
to come back, tomorrow, begging
for more. She had real work to do.

GOOD INTENTIONS

There were demons in the trees waiting
to drop into our unguarded souls. Words
let them in and words could keep them out
if we would only listen. Some rode in
to our homes on the backs of black cats, squelched
beneath wine corks, or hidden in the silence
that follows too many questions. The greatest
of them was a fallen singer which reminded us
not to let ourselves be swayed by the rhythms
of the world. Others lorded over flies, putting
any corpse to envy. There were demons
for every sin, and sins for every thought,
all of us cowering in the lights, afraid
the shadows would reach into our hearts
and find themselves at home.

DWI

They pulled Dad over on the way home
from visiting us at Aunt Louise's house
where we were staying while the divorce

went through. His truck died, so he shut
off his lights, cranked it, and flipped
them back on. A cop thought it was a signal

cause there had been robberies in the neighborhood.
When they brought him in, he informed
the whole building what he'd like for breakfast,

how his cell should be decorated. A preacher
came to talk. "Do you save people?" Dad
asked. "Yes sir," the preacher said, serious.

"Do you save women?" Dad asked.
"Yes sir," the preacher said, a touch of pride,
this time. "Do you save prostitutes?" Dad asked.

"Yes sir," the preacher nodded. "Well can you
save me a couple for Saturday night?" Dad asked.

BREAD CRUMBS

My brother's soul was all vermilion and fried
chicken, grease stains sweated through his aura
and dribbled behind him like the path of a slug.
I tried to walk in his footsteps, slipped and slid

behind him, sometimes to the ground, sometimes
right into his back. He would turn, grab my arm,
and lift me up like so much laundry in the air. Up
there I could see his bald patch, eggs in the bird's

nest in the ceiling of our porch who thanked their
mothers they were born sparrow, gnawed bones
spread over miles like the corpses of winds. He
would set me down, hold me until I was steady,

my arm in the air saluting, then turn, plod forward
and never fall. There were children in foreign lands
starving for what fell from him, starving for the air
he ate like chocolate.

LEVEES ALWAYS LEAK

The well spewed water from an alien-seeming white
PVC pipe into the green-topped rice field. We thought
it'd flow forever. In a hundred plus degree weather,
the mist was a Godsend. Sometimes, we'd back
a tractor up to a nearby pond and run a relift
to pump water out to a scorching field; we'd stand
under the thin sprays from leaks in the rubber pipe
trying to get cool, already soaked from sweat anyway.

White dirt levees snaked along high ground, sectioning
the field to spread the water evenly through plastic-lined
spillways, but the levees always leaked. We spent
sweltering afternoons wading in to shovel mud
into flowing water, patching or cutting new spillways.
When you drove by, they looked like they were running,
kaleidoscopic. Mosquitos rippled above them like mirages.

The smell of coolness, mud and water. The taste
of clean mud, well-water, rice chaff on the tongue.
Sun blistered the skin if it wasn't already burned red.
Old men cruised the shoulders, scanning levees, seeing
something I couldn't see.

I NEVER DID

Muddy water thick with roots and a semblance
of banks that drifted with the rains, leveed off
here and there into a brackish pond; all the field
runoff around flowed into the Languille River,
before joining the Mississippi, which meant
the catfish were fat and easy. We'd hang
a cane pole over the bushes when we were bored
on rainy days or after the crops were checked,
or set an aluminum boat to drift between lily pads
and stumps, more often than not hooking trotlines
long abandoned, gar with razor teeth, or old turtles.
If we'd thought about what went in there,
we wouldn't have eaten any of it. I used to collect
the oversized hooks in the bottom of my tackle box,
thinking I'd set my own trotline someday.

STRAW

Over by the vehicle shed: a sea of itchy
yellow tubes each taller than we were.

We'd clamber up one and run across
them, playing king of the mountain,

then drop into the gaps between to play
hide and seek in the softening bales. Snakes,

rats, and who knew what else lived
in the rotting green-going-yellow straw,

but we didn't care. Whenever Dad
or Uncle Bobby brought a tractor over

to spear one and haul it to the pasture
to feed the cows, we'd scatter before they

could yell at us, trying to hold our ragged breath
until they left and we could play again.

CUTTING BULLS

We'd had to separate three great, black angus
bulls due to their irascible natures. Taller
than me, tall as Dad, they seemed. We cut
the smallest and got it into the iron chute
on the far side of the pen. It was all I could do
to hold the handle down, the sides squeezing
its neck in place as it shuddered, threatening
to tear the whole thing apart while Dad treated it
and we let it kick loose. I headed for the other
young one on the far side, when the old one
caught sight of me. Half again as big as the others,
he stepped in front, nostrils flaring wide to suck
in my smell. His stone hoof ripped loam loose,
and he lowered his thick neck and ran at me. Dad
was there, between us, without even seeming
to move. I backed to the fence, trying not to run.
Dad stood his ground as the bull ran up
and stopped half-a-dozen feet short. It made
another feint, and another, each time stopping
a little further away. When it was tired out,
Dad backed it to the race that led to the chute.
I stepped up to hold the bar. When we'd finished
the last one, we headed back to the truck.
"If you'd run," Dad said, casual, like he was talking
about the weather, "He'd a tore your ass up."

THE NEW POND

A tornado knocked down the tin
shack we stored chemicals in, dumping
old poison, fertilizer, oil, who
can remember what into the white dust.

We figured more room to store the fish
we kept in vats in the south shed might cut
down on floaters, so we backhoed
a pit and bulldozed dirt up in a square

on the edge of the east field where the shed
once stood—we grew winter wheat, corn,
even grapes, there, once upon a time—trucked
in water and filled it with fingerlings

that were all floating in a couple days.
We scooped them out, buried them to cut
the smell, and started a series of experiments
based on the often drunken assertions

of passersby, involving dumping various
chemicals into the water, usually when
we were drunk, ourselves. We didn't know
what was killing them and didn't want

to waste the money restocking it over
and over, so folks would bring whatever
strange fish they caught and didn't want:
bowfins, grass carp, drums, gars, even

turtles. Nothing we could sell. Trout,
bass, crappies, and the like floated within
a day, but the trash fish survived. Eventually,
bullfrogs sang. Nobody'd eat them.

THE FIRST TIME

I was seven. Mom was back
from St. Louis waiting to die slow
from Huntington's Disease, living
in a hotel. My sister and I had been
staying with our aunt while they got
the divorce lined out. The family got
together like it was Thanksgiving. All
the aunts brought food. Everybody talked
nonstop and nobody said a word. Maybe
it was because I'd always been afraid
of water, its depth that could mask itself
as survivable. I went out to Aunt Louise's
pool, climbed in. I couldn't float, so I stood
on the bottom, turned toward the house to wait.
They'd followed me out, the whole family,
aunts, uncles, cousins, siblings gathered
around the edge. I could see their mouths
moving as they talked but heard only
the roar of water's silence.

RED

I wanted a dog because that's what boys
do. Dad bartered a redbone puppy
from a buddy and let me keep it outside,
ostensibly to teach it to hunt, as soon
as I learned, myself. I bugged him to help me
build a house for it, but every night, he rolled
in too pissed to hold a hammer. Afternoons,
after school, I'd climb the long hill, and Red
would launch himself at my head, knocking
me down. He liked to chase my sister's cat
from her food until she swiped him a good
one on the nose. We could've been any other
boy and his dog.
                    Dad came in drunk
a few days after we brought Red home, said
he saw a skunk outside, and went to shoot it.
I heard the rifle's report, then a long silence.
A while later, Dad came back in, even redder
faced. He went to bed and wouldn't speak.
The next morning, Red was gone.

CANTALOUPE

He'd cool it in the fridge after
buying it from the glaring old

man's roadside stand, halve
the cantaloupe, scoop the seeds

with a spoon, tossing them out
the door into the ditch the sink

and washing machine drained into,
douse one half with pepper, and eat

it to the green bone of the rind.
That was breakfast, along with

coffee, or, after he decided
that made him too jittery, Gatorade.

He'd read a Tom Clancy novel
in the kitchen until the sun was up,

and leave a rind in the sink so clean,
fruit flies wouldn't touch it.

SEINING

We called the big stock pond The Lake. It stretched
from the old WPA levee, alongside the gravel
pit, to another levee that separated it from a drainage
pond on the south end, and then petered out into marsh.

The pump sent the water pouring out into the drainage
ditch on the other side of the levee until The Lake shrank
to the size of a pond, then, a handful of guys would set
out in their hip waders to seine it.

The trick is that you can't stop walking or you'll sink.
The mud sucked at feet with hungry slurps. They'd drag
the net across the muddy water and slop and splurt
their way to the bank. A tractor with a basket was braced

on the shore. They had to separate the channel cats from mud
cats, any other odd fish or other things that had ended
up in the nets. The catfish would go into a fish tank
in the back of a pickup truck to be hauled to the shed

where they kept the larger tanks, soon, to be sold
to customers. Seagulls lined the banks to eat the mud
cats or whatever else was thrown in the grass and dirt
to die. You could smell the rotting fish all over the valley.

COWS ARE OUT

The phone rarely roused dad from his drunk.
It would be me or my sister who answered
the sheriff's call to tell us the cows were out.
After we woke him, most of the time, Dad
would just go back to bed saying they'd find
their own way back in. On a good night,
he'd struggle on pants, grab one of us if he
couldn't rouse our older brother, and drive
over to Killough Road. Sometimes, the gate
would be open or the fence would be down
from people breaking in to fish the stock
pond or hunt shrooms in the pasture.
The cows usually only wandered a little ways
down the road. We'd get out and ease toward
them to herd them back to the gate. There was
no need to wave or yell, just walk. The world
was quiet at 2 a.m. as they lowed softly,
calmer now that we were there, and clomped
on the asphalt, heading home.

ETIQUETTE

A pocket knife is a universal eating
implement. To clean, simply unfold
and wipe grease, gunk, etc. on a pant
leg, preferably before using. Wipe

and refold when finished. Vienna
sausages can be speared directly
from the can, placed on a stale saltine
cracker, and eaten in one bite. Potted

meat can be spread, similarly. Lunchmeat
is neither ham nor turkey but some strange
lesser cousin that costs half as much. Fish
it out of the cooler, drain the water

from the package, then place the thin, gray
slices on wadded-up white bread that's
been sitting in the truck for who knows
how long and yet is still soft. When you're

done, toss the detritus into a nearby ditch
or the back of the truck so it can spill out
as you drift along the highway at twenty- five
miles per hour, a line of angry cars following.

HOW TO RECYCLE A FARM TRUCK

A bumper can be replaced with a railroad tie, a barrel
welded to the front end, or simply dropped. A tailgate

more often gets in the way, best to take it off and stick
some plywood in its place if needed. A rusted bed can

be rebuilt with wood or steel or replaced with a slightly
less rusted bed. Doors can be mixed and matched or done

without. Windows are optional and may be replaced
with black garbage bags. The actual pedals for the brake

and gas are optional; likewise, rearview mirrors and rear
windows, mufflers, glove compartments. Dashboards.

Roofing nails and duct tape will fix most cosmetic issues
on the interior or under the hood. If required, feel free

to replace the engine with any that comes to hand. This
may require cutting the body to fit and removing the hood.

A wagon should never be bought, rather cut from a truck
that's beyond repair, if one can imagine such a thing.

THE FISH SHACK

There's no sign, just a gravel parking lot
leading to an open door, a concrete floor dark
as mud, the thud of knives on cutting boards.
Customers pick fish—cat or buffalo—from a tank
out front for us to weigh up and clean. A man
breaks out a harmonica while he waits. Another day,
a man brings his guitar, plays "Long-Haired Doney,"
Well my trouble, soon'll be over. Every time someone
comes in, they ask him to play, so he never gets
to order. He comes back the next day and does it
again. Outside, dust itches the throat, smells
of bone. Somebody gets drunk and tries to find water
with a divining rod, walks into the stock pond,
and says, "I told you it works." In the garden
across the lot, customers can pick greens while
they wait. They come in pairs, so one can watch
to make sure we don't try to slip frozen fish
in with the fresh. Which we would. The battered
radio hums country music no one can hear over
the laughter, the practical jokes. "Have you fed
the mongoose today, Bobby? Y'all ain't seen
our mongoose?" Everyone knows there's no
mongoose until the lid flies open and the fur-
covered tennis ball flies out. *Trouble will make you
sad for your Mama.* Evenings, Dad and them
stand around drinking and telling stories
none of them believe.

13 WAYS OF LOOKING AT A RICE FIELD

after Wallace Stevens

1. The levees are low walls. I stepped
over, but I still see mud
in my tracks all these years later.

2. Dragonflies hover over the feast,
like the helicopter Uncle Wheelbarrow stole,
set down in a rice field drunk
and hurting.

3. It's not water; it's the sweat
of generations from which grows
a momentary cessation of the banker's hostility.

4. A soft smell something like sweet
straw and mud,
a mother's hair.

5. Driving to college on a lonely highway,
levees race to catch up.

6. Blackbirds laugh from power lines
by the road as we trudge into the mud,
half-a-dozen spills and a shovel
on our shoulders.

7. Up on the high dirt road, somebody's
truck eases to a stop to wait until we're done.

8. My father took my fiancé on a tour of the rice
fields and told her, "Didn't know
you were marrying into landed gentry,
did you?"

9. The wind pushes flames across
the stubbled dirt. I watch
from the road, yearning for something
I can't name.

10. Weeds grow inside an old farmhouse.
A rusted bedframe just visible
through the window hole.

11. When mom got too sick to stay home,
they put her in a nursing home built where
we used to farm.

12. Dad would wade out with a shoulder
full of spills and a shovel in a hundred degree
heat, patch the levees that needed it and cut
others, then back at the truck, down
a Budweiser like it was water.

13. Mosquitoes nudge ears, nose, mouth,
the wind's reminder: yes, there is life in us,
if only we can get it out.

MUD

It'll suck you in if you slow
down. Each step, a throaty
release of rubber coming free
of deep mud. A line of men pulling
a net across the darkness
to gather catfish, buffalo fish,
dumpgulls circling overhead.
All of them working on
hangovers from the night before.
This is how bodies are broken,
not with a crack but a slow push.
I was afraid if I stepped in too deep,
I'd never get free.

IT WAS QUIET, THERE

The older kids fought for the backseats
where the bus driver couldn't see. They stole,
punched, threatened worse. We thought

they were tough because they chewed
tobacco, dipped, carried condoms in their
back pockets that wore a ring into the denim.

As long as they didn't get loud, the driver
didn't care; they were football players, rich
kids. The junior high was only a few

miles from my house, so I walked most days
through the stream that bordered the school,
the patch of woods full of sticker bushes.

HE NEVER BOTHERED ME AGAIN

Cece Frankenstein was the oldest girl
on the bus. My sister's friend, every day
she'd say hi, but embarrassed by her blond

hair and pretty smile, I'd mumble nothing
as she walked away. Bobby Parsons and some boys
cornered me when she'd disappeared down

the long walk to her house on the edge of my family's
land. "What are you doing talking to Cece?" Bobby
asked. He challenged me to a fight and didn't

show but told the other kids on the bus it was me
who wimped out. Every day, when Cece was out
of sight, they'd follow me, shoving and picking,

until one afternoon, I finally turned, kicked Bobby hard
between the legs. He went down, and the others
scattered. His eyes closed and he didn't even moan.

I cut and ran for the Fish Shack, in tears, thinking
I'd killed him. My brother asked if I'd been
in a fight, and all I could say was, "Sort of."

COWS

There's something in the steady grind of grass
between blunt teeth that hints at infinity.
The brush of incisors through green hairs, nipping

their tips off to chew and swallow, regurgitate
and chew. The cow's sounds blanket the heart in direct
opposition to the lonesome wail of the train's call

as it passes, the bug chatter threatening to consume
the night. How could anything that makes
such soothing sounds not be wise? A cow

will lie down when it's full, stand and chew
when it's not. Millennia of debate between the wisest
men have produced nothing as simple or profound.

TEA

We have a black & white picture: a lewdly smiling
young almost-Ronald Reagan in uniform in a Japanese

cathouse with two unnamed, bug-eyed boys.
"That's why I've always associated tea with sex,"

he'd explain. He'd joined up after his older brother
Wayne's plane crashed taking out kamikaze. They'd

buried Wayne in France where his hard-scrabble
mother could never afford to visit. "At least that way
I got to see the grave," Dad said. "They wanted me

to be an officer, but I just wanted to go home." The war
ended for my father on a ship halfway to the Pacific

Theater. With a belly full of cheap bourbon,
he'd talk about trading KP or guard duty

for others' beer allotment. Once, after a friend passed,
he mentioned how a bunch of them had hopped

a truck to see what Fat Man left of Nagasaki.
"I'm probably the only one left that saw it," he said.

WAR WITH KOREA

We lost. Ask the factory workers
who've given up even looking
for work. Maybe moved in with Dad.

Maybe found a doctor willing
to put us on disability. Maybe
just sitting at home until they

wheel us out. Here, things break down
slightly slower than they used to. Someone
somewhere else bought an island.

A BOY AND HIS DOG

I don't remember why I looked outside,
but there Dad was, his beaten-down, once-black
Ford pulled over in the tall grass, up the road
toward the top of the hill. I went to meet him,
thinking anything would be better than
the boredom inside. When I was closer, I could see
he had his snake rifle aimed at a dog running
across the far side of the valley. I knew
what he was thinking: the dog had been spooking
the cows, might incite them to hurt
themselves. So he was taking the practical
solution. A rise blocked him from seeing
the boy climbing the other side of the ridge, up
from Aunt Mary Bob's trailer, chasing
his dog that'd gotten out. And I ran,
trying to beat that crack of thunder that
travelled miles faster than I ever could.

WE NAMED HIM SMEAGOL BECAUSE OF HIS BUG EYES

Dad came in liquored up, grumbling
because the spindly kitten my sister had gotten
for me the week before had pissed

the carpet. He snatched it in one hand, leaned
out the utility room door, and smacked its head
against the red bricks on the front of the house

one, two, three times. I tried to run at him, knock
him the rest of the way out, like he wouldn't
have bashed me against the same wet spot.

My sister grabbed me while he threw its limp
body in the tall grass on the edge of the open
sewage pipe coming from the kitchen.

I didn't talk to him for three days. He asked
my sister what was wrong with me. "I'm not
sure," she said, her eyes wide with fear.

THE PATH

I hit Junior High, already too bored to ever
care about graduating. After class, we'd go out
to the ragged gravel roads, cruise around

in my sister's second Toronado that wouldn't reverse,
and smoke thin joints, trying to open ourselves
to something resembling joy. At first, I didn't know

how to inhale, so she'd shotgun me until my greed
taught me. We were hopeless, poor sons and daughters
of already dying men and women without even

the spark of hate to goad them on. My sister
made all the drug dealers promise they wouldn't sell
to me. She'd take me to our cousins who'd already

settled into their graves, just staring up at the sky,
with their loosening teeth, psychotic parents, neglected
lives; this was the path of too much joy, all the preachers said.

JOHNSON'S FREEZE INN

By Mad Dog Liquor, across from the old
CMS chemical factory, just past the grey

arc of asphalt where 64 hits 1, a plywood
shack barely big enough to swing a cat in,

with a menu painted on a board offering anything
that could be battered and deep fried in lard

who knows how old. My favorite was a double
bacon cheeseburger, slathered in mustard

with diced onions no matter how you asked
for it, with dripping cheese sticks served on greasy

paper, along with a Styrofoam cup of butterscotch
milkshake you couldn't even suck through the straw.

You wouldn't spend five bucks on the lot,
but it was so much better than anywhere else

with a name. You circled through the gravel
and broken concrete of the lot and waited

till the old woman was ready, paid with cash,
and didn't ask too many questions, or she'd slide

the window closed and you didn't get fed.

FROGBALL

We couldn't afford bats so we scavenged
broken lengths of PVC pipes, crooked

sticks, hands, if that's all we had. Likewise,

instead of baseballs we used pinecones, dried
cow pies, rocks. One kid started catching

frogs and smacking them into trees. We envied
his easy swing in duct-taped shoes, home-

cut hair, and worn-out clothes. None of us
were frogs so we didn't protest too much

other than to let him always take bat when
he caught one. We hardly went to his house,

anyway, with its collapsing roof, gun-collecting,
drug-addled mom's boyfriend. At least

he wasn't burying cats and mowing their heads
off, diddling his sister, or telling us we'd, all of us,

never escape the burning lake we were born for.

HARD TIMES, ARKANSAS

They weren't all bad, those angry years.
I've mostly forgotten the taste of sawdust

meant to keep the belly from swelling too
noticeably, though the smell of want

on my own skin never quite washes away.
There was laughter, not all at my own

expense, though I was a dancing monkey
when I smelled change, I admit. There

were days when she smiled and danced
in her panties when no one could see

but me. There was fire in the veins
and the gut. Genius spat into camp

fires. Drugs were cheap and plentiful
and none of us had obligations in the morning.

There was no tomorrow, in Hard Times,
so why bother? All of our fathers hated

the sight of us the same, so no one felt
slighted. All of us would've helped bury

a body for the others, though none of us
owned a shovel. Still, we were used

to stealing from hardware stores.

HONORS ENGLISH

I'd forgotten my textbook
in a friend's car. My English
teacher asked, "Why didn't you

get a ride to retrieve it?"
I didn't answer, from whom?
My mother who no longer

knew her own name, drugged and locked
away in a nursing home?
My father, who spent his nights

out late and angry drunk? "You
give up too easily," she
said. It had been two slow weeks

since I'd tasted the cold oil
and metal of the rifle

in my mouth and tried to think
of a reason not to squeeze.

GUARDIANS

You've always been a ghost,
to me, rooted to the hall carpet's cheap
brown fuzz, the whale song
of your intentions littering the background
of my life like yesterday's socks
when I wish, I wish I could only
hear it hum. Maybe you trained crows
to scour the sides of highways for tossed
coins, love notes blown from messy
cars, with the intention of sharing
these things. Maybe you were the one
who was brave enough to swim
to the stratosphere when the heavy
winds came, but could not teach me
to keep my arms up. You loved
and were loved long before I ever
appeared. I'm grateful for this.
There could be no greater horror
than the dead watching over the lives
they can no longer help.

THIRSTY

Dad started the mornings at the Fish Shack
with a finger of Kentucky Tavern bourbon

in the bottom of a solo cup topped off
with water. When he'd drained that, he put in

two fingers, then four. As the liquid darkened,
his hat crept back on his head revealing salt

and pepper hair, and the amount of fuck he gave
dried up like water in the sun. In the summers,

he'd wade out into a rice field in a hundred
degree weather, come back to the truck to down

a Budweiser seemingly in one gulp, and then head
back into the water. Uncle Lonnie got cirrhosis

and filled empty vodka bottles with water so
nobody noticed. I'd steal drinks from unattended

cups when I was a kid, later, beers from Dad's
cooler. Across the tracks, they'd sell to you if you went

through the drive through, one of you in the back
seat playing loaded already, barking orders at the driver.

MY FATHER, DRIVING

He drove so slow, Death
got out to walk.

* * *

It saves on cleaning,
because he doesn't raise dust.

* * *

Everybody was so friendly;
they all waved, but real
cool-like with just one finger.

* * *

Sometimes, he liked to race old
Grampa Taylor; he usually
won now that Grampa was dead.

* * *

Hard to tell if he's going
forwards or backwards until
somebody lays on the horn.

* * *

When the horizon comes up
too fast, he gets scared he might
fall off the Earth and miss supper.

WALLOW

The aunts called to ask why Dad's truck
was sitting in the road, twenty-five yards

from the house, door open. My brother
and I found him, passed out in a grass wallow.

A trail led up to the rusted, mostly black door
where he'd crawled back to get the rest

of his muscadine wine. We dragged him
to the truck, coasted down to the house,

and dumped him in bed. The aunts
began to appear hours later with casseroles,

desserts, accusations. When they left,
it was quiet. He slept and we ate our fill.

Doing His Best

When they put mom in the nursing home, Dad
laid on the couch for three days to sweat all

the liquor out. When we rolled the stone aside,
he had plans. I got braces to fix my smile,

hunting trips to fix my manhood. When I was
a baby, he'd sit up, nights, in the rocking chair

while mom slept. He called me sweetie for years,
until I grew into a thing he didn't understand. Then,

he went back to work. Being a man meant keeping
a roof over his family's heads, keeping us fed.

Understanding wasn't part of the bargain. With Mom
gone, Dad would make big messes of beans, fry

chicken that still bled on the paper towel. He'd call
me from reading in my room to come peel potatoes.

He visited her every day, stopping by on the way home.
The house filled with shadows, the quiet broken by TV.

SHOES

You wore duct-taped shoes, had holes
in everything, ripped and raggedy scarecrow.
A teacher saw and bought you a stylish new
pair, and when you got them home,
your mom's boyfriend stole them. Your dad

was serving life in Texas for gun-running,
multiple man-slaughters. You hadn't seen him
in years and didn't plan to. Your mom pleaded
out to raise you and your four siblings, until
she got bored and ran off with a trucker.

You lived with your grandmother for that year
in a clean house in Parkin. Somehow,
that was worse than the slowly collapsing
cabin by the lake. Dirty doesn't have expectations,
I guess, or raise them. I met you in junior high.

Lanky and brave, always with a smile. Strong
as a poet. Best friend I'd ever had. We wasted
our lives together. When your mom stole all your stuff,
I begged my dad until he took you in. I taught you
how to drink so well you never drank again.

THE WATER MOCCASIN'S MOUNTAIN

Rice levees follow high ground to keep the most
water in with the least dirt. They gerrymander

across the fields, broken by orange spills, smell
like mud and something sweet I can't explain.

I'd slosh after Dad, hauling spills and a shovel,
too focused on not falling to even look.

There was too much work to do for him to wait
for me to figure out how to shovel right. Mostly,

I sat in the truck wondering if Dad would hear
if I shot that laughing crow off the power line.

Sometimes, he'd set me to pull coffee weeds
on layout ground to keep me occupied. Otherwise,

it wasn't that hard to figure out how to start
an old farm truck with a flathead screwdriver.

WHITE BEANS

Soak the beans overnight in salty water,
rinse out any dirt or detritus, and drain.
The salt water will make them softer, later.
Beans go in a pot with chicken stock, or a hunk

of ham. A good beer or even wine could
work, depending on what you add later
to compliment. Season as though your tongue
has lived a life of sullen isolation and this

is your one chance to wake it up to a world
it has never known. This includes pepper,
some bay leaves if you actually believe
those do anything other than make you choke

when you accidentally eat one, and remember
that the ham is probably salty enough
already. Black pepper. Red pepper. Chunk
up an onion, several garlic cloves. Kale

or some kind of green will help balance
the sweetness of the beans, especially
if you added beer. The thing about beans
is you can add anything to them and it'll only

make them better; they are the ultimate egalitarian
dish. Now add more ham. Plan to boil them
all day until they're on the verge of mush
but not past that. The broth should be thick.

The beans should be soft. If they're not,
keep cooking. Once they're done, taste them,
and add more pepper. Serve with cornbread,
a couple hunks of sharp cheddar. Hot sauce.

THE WIZARD

If baseball is America, then America
is Ozzie Smith. *No. 1, man on fire*
doing backflips across the field,
more magic than mountain. My big brother

and I would make the trip to St. Louis once
a year—a five-hour drive that took
us two days round trip—stay in a cheap
motel, me always scrunching down

in the car and then sequestered in the room
so the management wouldn't charge us
for two. Feasting on the same fast food
from different joints, uncomfortable seats

under a sweat-inducing sun, and people almost
as strange as us, until The Wizard took the field
with a handstand. *Go crazy, folks, go crazy!*

An agitated atom in a field of static forms.
We were there to see perfection; if Ozzie
couldn't catch it, it couldn't be caught.

THE ONE-EYED KING'S LAMENT

Mother, a screaming shadow, father, drunk
in a field somewhere; I had no one to warn me
how rough the knuckles of idiocy could grow

from all that dragging. I was soft, looking to smile
in the rain and swim in the snow while they plopped
on the couch for the weather report. I wanted to think

I won because I got away, but every time I see
their graves on a map, my ears burn, my nostrils
twitch. Not even their worms remember me.

WALMART

After my sister got the job sewing crotches
at the jeans factory, there was no one to smoke
pot with after school, so I'd walk over

to the Walmart a block from the junior high,
past the welfare apartments, and steal things.
I wore a loose coat with a hole in the pocket

that opened into the lining. There were two aisles
where cameras couldn't see, over by the ceiling
fans. The employees didn't care what anyone did.

I'd steal baseball cards, comic books, candy, anything
that wasn't so expensive they'd notice.
If I had any money, maybe I'd buy some gum

or a soda, and carry it all out through the line.
Half the time, it was obvious the checker saw
the bulges in my coat, but they never stopped me.

I'd go out to the quarter operated kiddie carousel
or the knock-off soda machines and hide my spoils,
then back in for another round for the hour it took

my sister to come pick me up. She'd talk about cast-
offs with three legs, a woman who sewed her fingers
together, the machine's needle having punctured to

the bones. They had surprise drug tests so she could
never smoke anymore. One time a manager came out
and found my backpack full of stuff. I watched him

from the arcade games in the lobby. He opened the bag
up, peeked in, and looked around but didn't see me.
He left it there and went inside. I grabbed it

and high-tailed it to the far end of the strip mall to wait.
The next day, I found a new hiding place.

TO THE POLICEMAN WHO CALLED ME MA'AM

Over the years, I've told this story more than once:
how a cop asked my buddy if he was taking his girlfriend

on a date, though I had a full beard and nothing feminine
about me except long hair. We knew the only reason

he pulled us over was the college decal. Folks would call us
'college boys' and sneer as though we didn't know

what it was to be trapped. Every time I wore a sweater
someone would threaten to kick my ass for being queer.

Another policeman, months later, pulled me over to ask
if I was in 'one of them cults out of Memphis.' I ran away

because I was born among men who didn't know how to dream.
But if I don't challenge you on this, who will challenge you

on anything? I've had just a taste of harassment. Others live
their days in fear of the thumb smooshing down. The simple

fact is that I cut my hair, that I don't wear sweaters.
There never was a cult out of Memphis. It didn't need one.

HUFFING POTPOURRI WHILE LISTENING TO TOOL

I didn't realize I would never love anyone
as much as I loved you then, damaged

and stoned as you were but surrounded
by light. Your sex tasted perfect, salty

and sweet, blood and mud; it's not something
I can put into words. I didn't know

what whole was, but I wanted you safe,
smiling, far away from those
who could hurt you like I did.

NIGHTS WERE LONG

You drove gravel roads, barely paved single lanes, long
forgotten highways that were more pothole than asphalt,
drinking double-deuces, smoking whatever you could
find. Prescription meds stolen from geriatric relatives
could be crushed and snorted. If you could afford meth,
you could smoke it off aluminum foil if you remembered
to burn the coating off first. Booze and weed
were usually available. If nothing else, you could steal
half-a-dozen cans of potpourri from Walmart and huff
them through a towel. Otherwise, it was church eight
days a week, dropping out of high school to farm
or work a factory that would close in a couple years
anyway. You weren't wasting your time; you were
looking for love at the end of an emptied-out pen,
the bottom of a beer can with holes punched through
the side and a carburetor poked in the bottom so you
could smoke when you didn't have papers.

I WAS THIN, THEN, AND YOUNG

The phone rang all hours, on the other end,
a television set, light breathing, a hint of sex.
I'd read cereal boxes, poems, tell jokes until
I made her laugh, and she'd hang up. I wore

my hair long and black, which invited fists,
tee shirts I could never find now, my jeans painted
with flowers because why the hell not? I played
guitar and sang badly, and had no idea anyone

could ever value me, even when anonymous
poems came in the mail. I didn't know it was love,
when girls whispered when they saw me. I thought
they were just softer fists. All around me was hate

and stupidity, and so how could anything beautiful
thrive? I had a lot of friends, so people assumed
I was a drug dealer. I was flattered they'd think
I was so ambitious. So much was wasted. They

didn't want to know anything different lest
the devil steal their shriveled hearts. I just didn't
realize life could ever get worse than this.

THE YELLOW KING

Everything smelled like grease, even
on your day off. I worked there for two
days. On the first, a coworker got into
an argument with a plant in the lobby
while I was on lunch. It looked like
the plant got the better of him. When
I went back behind the counter, the shift
manager with the piercings in her cheek said
he wasn't violent. The others gathered around
her as she pontificated in mumbled slang
about high times in the trailer park.

I was going to New York the next day,
a trip I'd planned before getting the job.
I would eat my first veggie pizza—just bread
and plants, really—try calamari, drink six
dollar beer, be felt up by strangers in a city
where everyone wore black and hated
everything. Just because I would never be one
of them didn't mean I would ever only
be me. When I got back, I worked one
more day with the familiar smell
and the boredom. I took my shirts back
when I picked up my check. No one cared.
It happened all the time.

NEW YEAR'S DAY

One of the junkies in the backseat spoke
up to ask, "Should there be so much smoke

behind us?" A wall of gray poured from the car.
I took the first exit, wondering how far

I could make it before the explosion, no flames
yet. I found a Walmart, parked and tried to wake

my ex who just wanted to stay in her seat. I gave
up, went in, and asked them for help before the blaze

took out somebody else's car. They wouldn't even call
the fire department. Meanwhile, my passengers had all

been kicked out of the store for trying to make a pallet
in an aisle, pulling pillows and blankets out. Now that

I'd stopped driving, flames poured from my hood. I stood
and watched it burn. My ex took my hand, asked if I would

go inside and buy her some cigarettes, since she
was banned. "It's kind of funny," she said. I came back

to find a man spraying out the fire. He warned me
to be careful if I drove the car, since the battery

had melted from the flames. "Do you think it would turn
over?" I asked. "Well, no, just be careful. That acid burns

pretty bad." he said. "It can melt through most things".

SWEATER

Before the snow came, you picked
a sweater from my closet,
slipped it on without a word.

I knew it would replace me—
my smell, my shape—until you
finished grieving and threw it

out. We drove up to campus
for coffee. I watched the sky—
through the door—darken, you said,

like I thought a spurned husband
might crash in. You had so far
to go. I joked you could stay

if the mountain roads shut down,
but I knew we'd failed and you
weren't coming back. We walked to

the parking lot. I watched you
drive away. The fat flakes fell,
obliterating the sky.

EVERYTHING I KNOW ABOUT CHICKENS

1.

A girl I used to love who didn't love me had
a childhood friend whose father worked
at a chicken plant. All the spotted chicks
would be drowned, so she begged until her father
brought several home. In their new pen,
the chicks began to peck each other's spots,
their blood splattering, which gave them more spots
to peck, until all died but one. That one, she raised.

2.

My dad and uncles used to dredge out the old silage
at the bottom of the pit, which had lain, fermenting,
for months, shovel it into a bucket, and let the chickens
have at it until they stumbled and lurched
around the Fish Shack, mimicking their owners.

3.

Erma Bombeck once claimed, as a child, she taught
her pet chicken to walk backwards. Others have claimed
to teach theirs math.

4.

There are more varieties of chickens than people I've ever met.

5.

At my grandmother's house, they would spend
all day hopping and gliding from a stump
to the swing set to a small tree, but they rarely
got as high as the roof. They ranged free, the road
still gravel, mostly unused, though the odd car
did catch the more adventurous ones.

6.

Even a pig sty smells less offensive than a chicken coop.

7.

Chickens will de-infest a garden better than any herbicide,
and their feces will fertilize.

8.

The FDA designations of "cage free" and "free range"
do not, in fact, denote freedom or a lack of cages.

9.

On our third and final date, that wasn't really a date, we met
at a friend's farm. There was a pen with pullets of all
varieties. She sat in the grass, to let them come to her.
My daughter overcame her protectiveness and snuggled
beside her while I stood—separate—and watched them smile.

GRANDMA OKRA

It doesn't grow wild; who knows where
it came from, green and furry, full of seeds

like a primitive pomegranate. Some complain
about the slime but will suffer it in gumbo

if you don't point it out; egg-battered, dipped
in flour, and fried is the best way. A smattering

of onion, pepper, salt: it doesn't need much; the sharp

green peeks through if you don't over-season. Serve it
with a pork chop smothered in gravy, a side of white

beans with ham hock to taste, cornbread to sop it up
or maybe a ripe garden tomato sliced thick.

HOW TO COOK SQUIRREL

The best cut is the legs, a tough dark
meat, like chicken nuggets from a cheap
pizza place but without all the preservatives.

After Mom went into the nursing home,
Dad liked to have me deep-fry them whole
and wide-eyed so he could suck

out their eyeballs, a delicacy I never tried.
Squirrel and dumplings is best. One shot
to the head or heart. The fur comes off loose.

Three or four plump ones are enough to fill
a pot with tasty broth I haven't had since
I left for college.

AFTER HE SOBERED UP

Dad fired my brother that morning, came
home to tell me, "There's no future

in farming," so I better find something
else to do. My brother lay in his room

for months, making the odd road trip
to Tunica when he could borrow gas

money. I didn't leave the house for two
years. All we knew was rice and catfish,

soybeans and corn, long evenings bull-
shitting and draining bourbon bottles.

Our bosses might've been assholes,
but they were family.

My brother got a factory gig working
with vulcanized rubber at an OSHA-

exempt plant. He'd come home nearly
blind, eyes burning and too pissed

to drink. Dad sold all the cows. The grass
grew long and wild in the pasture. The stock

pond filled with snakes and trash fish.
Finally, I cut my hair, worked fast food

and grocery stores that didn't owe me
anything. Went to college and ended up

too far away from home to make it back.

A CLOUD OF BLACKBIRDS

They came for the corn. The sky,
a wave of black dots, static
on an old-timey television, but they
moved and flowed like they might cover
the sun. As they settled into the rows,
arrogant as landlords, their raucous cries
taunted us. Their feathers were black
peppered with gray like my father's hair.
I didn't know a word for beauty like theirs,
Fragile and alien, but ours were not hearts
open to sharing. We rented traps big
as trailers. The birds came through the top
to feed but couldn't escape. We got hundreds,
but they kept coming. We had to dump
them out, afterwards. Tiny black bodies,
strange and hard.

THE GRASS IN ARKANSAS

doesn't need wind to dance.
Tiny dark olive hands wave
you onward; though there are snakes,
ticks, holes deep enough to wrench
an ankle, there's no choice but to run.

* *

The sun dozes just above your shoulder,
leeching the green from everything.
Cows nip the grasses' tips and chew
for hours.

* *

Hills exist to run down
too fast to stop at the bottom.
The legs are scourged clean;
in a similar way, the thoughts.
If you pause long enough, you'll hear
the susurrations of the dead, begging.

ELVIS

Mom says she's pregnant and Elvis
is the father. She'd met him once,
before he'd hit big, playing a gig
at the teacher's college. Back then,
she was a sorority beauty queen.

The nurses clip pictures from magazines,
young Elvis, old Elvis. They tape them up
above her bed. When we visit, she calls
all her children's names in quick
succession, as though she can't remember
who belongs to which name.

THE LESSON

My father taught me a certain kind
of fear that swelled, like water rushing in

to fill any empty space. He packed
his hours with mud to keep it out—so much,

you'd think he could've made a man
from the tracks left in the laundry room—

his nights with the bitter burn of cheap bourbon,
which is, granted, another kind of liquid.

The secret he knew: despair is a weak thing,
stove up and give out from that hard burden;

it can't wade as far into Arkansas mud
as a rice farmer, slooshing his leg free and pitching

it forward to sink again into the rot so old
it smells like clean. Sometimes, you've got

to laugh to keep from crying. Sometimes,
you've got to walk to keep from falling down.

JACKSON

My cousin said her daddy was doing things
to her, so I got a buddy to drive us to her mother's
apartment in Jackson when she was supposed

to be at school. She brought along her best friend,
another distant cousin. We rode in my buddy's
diesel, thundering all the way, talking about

the kind of tripe teenage boys say to girls. The friend
scooted up to my buddy along the way. My cousin
looked at me, said something about me playing guitar,

and I looked away. We dropped her off to wait
for her mom to get home from work, headed back
across state lines hoping to get the friend back

before school was over. They dropped me off
at home, and an hour passed before people started

coming to the door to ask where the girls were.
I thought my buddy had taken the friend back,
but they were parked out on some gravel road.

The cops came after dark to search the house.
My father woke to cuss them about how my cousin's
step-mom called me a devil worshiper but shacked up

with a man she wasn't married to. It shocked me.
I wondered why my cousin hadn't called her dad
while they searched the house. The friend was home

by then but wouldn't say where she'd been. I sat up
that night, reading the bible, hoping, though I knew
it was false hope, that a good deed would be honored.

CROSSWORD

He sits on the loveseat's edge,
TV blaring reruns he
didn't watch the first time, can't

hear them anyway, and scribbles
answers to the crossword. It
takes him two, sometimes three days.

When he finishes, he sets
that paper aside, looks all
around the room as if for

the first time seeing the walls
painted bright since the rebuild
after the fire, the kids'

pictures long gone, as they are.
He grabs the next day's paper,
sharpens his pencil, and lowers

his eyes back to the black
and white page.

STRENGTH

Mom shrank in fluorescent light,
her mind the withering pulp
of an aging apple, but she

couldn't die. I had no way
to comfort her ghost that wailed
outside my bedroom door each night

until my head broke from lack
of sleep, so I did what they said
would fix it, sat and chatted

with a dozy man about all the toothy
things that hid in the edges of my sight.
No one would ever love me

again. No one ever had,
maybe. Who can know such things?
With all the pills I couldn't afford

but took each day until years
had passed, I learned how to sleep
during rain, stood in the sun

when I could. There was always
work to be done. Steps to count
that might lead somewhere better.

MUSIC

You come in late on purpose, long enough
that the ushers have taken their seats, sit
in the back so only the most devout turn
to see. You're uncomfortable, not just
because the pews are harder than you
remember, but because you do remember
that you were never comfortable, here,
and whatever you thought was familiar
was a memory of something that never
happened. An old man talks. He cares
more about the evils of the world
than you have ever cared for the good.
People cough, fidget. You begin to understand
that they are not comfortable, either,
but they stay, and so do you, this one time.
Your mother felt something, here. Maybe you
could feel something of her, but your worry
is that it was only fear or habit or a chance
to get out of the house. The man is working
himself into a passion about sin, about his fear
that the world is moving away from him,
and you realize, sitting there, a third
of your body numb, that you'd never considered
the movements of the world to be anything
other than music, a concerto to be listened to,
feared, affected by, but not one that can be
altered; only the way in which you listen
can change. Now, they sing, and you feel the end
coming. You stumble for the door, before
their curious hands can find yours, their mouths
asking if you'll be back next Sunday.

www.ingramcontent.com/pod-product-compliance
Lightning Source LLC
LaVergne TN
LVHW040204180726
843489LV00007B/2685